PRAISE F(

Rhonda Bratcher is a pioneer in her own right. She has an apostolic and a prophetic voice in the earth that lays foundations and shifts atmospheres. Her tears and her faith have been her fight, as she roared through disappointments, distractions and criticisms. She always lands on her feet. I'm proud of who God has called her to be. The Pioneer's Prophetic Prayer Journal will help unlock your journey into God's presence.

— Marie Mouzon,
Kingdom Worship Center, Towson, MD

Those who possess a prayer anointing and a prophetic mantle, to strategically hear from God and see what He is saying or doing, are targets for demonic attacks and the challenges that blind and create deafness. Gifted prayer warriors have stories of having to war with the Prince of Persia! This is no epiphany for those who are attracted to this journal. Rhonda Bratcher, like many of us, knows what it means when we say, "I must fight if I should reign; increase my courage, Lord!" She, like many of us, has scars of victory! Yet, none ever regret the path God chooses for them to take; they respond daily with thanksgiving for the grace they receive for every assignment. The Pioneer's Prophetic Prayer Journal will assist every weary traveler on their respective journey!

— Archbishop Ralph L. Dennis,
Kingdom Worship Center, Towson, MD

THE PIONEER'S
Prophetic Prayer Journal

RHONDA BRATCHER

THE PIONEER'S
Prophetic Prayer Journal

RHONDA BRATCHER

ISBN: 978-1-7356789-6-2 (Paperback)

Library of Congress Control Number: 2021908358

Title Your Truth Publishing
9103 Woodmore Centre Drive, Suite #334
Lanham, MD 20721
hello@titleyourtruthpublishing.com
www.titleyourtruthpublishing.com

DEDICATION PAGE

To my grandchildren Kamryn, Kyla, and Rodney who
will live out the words of this book in their future.

CONTENTS

INTRODUCTION

Sometimes it's hard to believe that this book was written over fifteen years ago. It is especially prophetic for such a book to emerge during a global pandemic! At the time, it wasn't fully clear to me that God had a plan that would materialize several years later—using me, as His scribe!

For years, I've regarded writing as a source of therapeutic strength. And when I wrote, God broke through my limited understanding to show me a new perspective of Who He is. I embraced every word from His Spirit, knowing it was not only a gift to receive, but also a privilege! During those moments of intimacy, I realized who I was and how I could be a vessel of hope for other prophetic pioneers— those who were struggling to realize and embrace their own unique calling.

Understanding who you are is paramount for changing the trajectory of your life and others who are directly impacted by your obedience. As an intercessor, you are one who intervenes on behalf of another. You are a mediator— one who stands in the gap. As a prophetic intercessor, you are one who receives insight from heaven concerning how to intervene on behalf of another before God. You are heaven's mouthpiece, as you not only stand in the gap on behalf of another, but release targeted prayers based upon heaven's revelation. As a pioneer, you are one who establishes, creates, and births what is new and nonexistent. You are a trailblazer— an innovator! As a prophetic pioneer, you are one who functions in a dimension that has yet to be revealed or known. You break forth what hasn't been and establish what is about to take place. So, as a prophetic intercessor and pioneer, it's time to make strategic moves!

Pioneering prophetic movements during this time is crucial. And in order to operate with accuracy and wisdom, we must understand our spiritual climate, as times and seasons are revealed. Understanding every intricacy of who you are and who God has called you to be aligns you with the fulfillment of His will, and sharpens your understanding of how to make movements more effectively. Therefore, it is my sincere prayer that you are able to utilize the pages of this prophetic prayer journal to help you explore God in a new way and become more keenly aware of His creative power in your life.

I pray that the Lord blesses you and fills you
until you overflow in Jesus name.
May the Lord enlighten the eyes of your heart.
I pray that the Lord opens your ears to hear
what His Spirit is saying to His church.
I pray that He heals every wounded spirit, soul, and body.
May He deliver the totality of your being
and bless you with spiritual truth.
May you receive God's revelation, illumination, impartation,
transformation, and manifestation in the Name of Jesus!
May total deliverance take place in your life,
renewing your mind completely.
May you receive total restoration, strength, joy,
peace, and prosperity in Jesus name. Amen.

THE SEED

THE SEED

Scripture

"Verily, verily, I say unto you, except a corn of
wheat fall into the ground and die, it abided alone:
but if it dies, it bringeth forth much fruit."
—John 12:24

Poem

There is a seed that lies dormant in man
This seed is a part of the Master's Plan
This seed was created by the spoken word
Its destiny never seen, its purpose never heard
It follows a process of falling into the ground
To come forth with greatness releasing a new sound
When it dies to the process of all it could take
This is when the seed realized it was awake

Reflection

A seed is potential, waiting to come forth
A seed is planted in soil, only for its growth
It goes through the process; it even has to die
It has to be the right climate
It needs the sun (Son) shining in the sky
As the seed dies, it also resurrects
Then it brings forth more than we expect
Seeds also breakthrough from the low places in the ground
Coming forth in acceleration, moving up elevating to a point
The seed has formed a root that keeps an anchor in the ground
To continue to grow, budding starts to take place
And we get a glimpse of our destiny
Storms and rain come for us to grow more and more
Then there is pruning that will leave you sore
Then there is dung that smells horrible, but necessary for growth
A seed is the beginning of your destiny in the earth
You are a seed that started as one, but
have bought forth many things
A seed is prophetic to me, it becomes more than what you see
The earth has to go through this process to embrace eternity
A finished spiritual product shows itself in time
through something tangible or visible

Affirmation

I am God's seed sent from heaven to bring forth
abundance and produce prophetic fulfillment.

Prophetic Preview

It's time to bring the prophetic out of you. Begin to worship the Lord and get in His presence. Listen closely for His voice and wait for Him to speak.
On the following page, journal your thoughts and impressions. Record every directive given. As heaven is revealed to you, begin to prophetically intercede.
Don't be limited to just words. Allow heaven to communicate to you through visuals. Additional space is provided for you to draw what heaven reveals to you.

Journal

Drawing Space

TAKING A JOURNEY
INTO THE 3RD DAY

TAKING A JOURNEY INTO THE 3RD DAY

Scripture

"Now when he had left speaking, he said unto Simon, launch
out into the deep, and let down your nets for a draught."
—Luke 5:4

Prayer Poem

Lord I thank you for releasing me
And then you've changed my clothes
You've placed a garment of authority upon me
For the whole world to know
Then you take me to a boat
And prepare me to set sail
Before we leave you remove the things
That would cause me to stumble or fail
I look up high to a dark sky
That appears to always be this way
As I focus intently
Something starts to hit me

That this night is becoming day
I start to anticipate in my heart
That this Light is shining through my night
As I set sail on this boat into Your Presence
You assure me that this travel is in Your way and might
Finally, we arrive to a Holy Place
And now I can truly see
That this is the path of righteousness
Launching me into the deep places of intimacy
The winds are blowing, I hear You speaking
And now I must obey
I thank you Lord for your perfect will
As I live in the habitation of the 3rd day

Reflection

Years ago, I had a vision that I was walking on the beach. I stepped into the water and began to walk out. Suddenly, a snake wrapped itself around me and took me deep into the water. The snake started to squeeze me tightly and take my head under the water. This happened three times. And from the heavens, lightning struck the water and hit the snake. Suddenly, it let me go. As I swam back toward the shore, Jesus was waiting for me; He pulled me from the water and changed my damped clothes. He put linen garments on me and walked me over to a boat. Before I entered the boat, people began to get off the boat. I asked the Lord: "Who are these people?" He replied, "These people represent spirits that cannot go with you on this journey." Imagine taking a journey in a vehicle with no space for extra items. So, I got on the boat and sat down; a big tide came in and lifted the boat turning it around to set sail into the deep. I journeyed until the early hours in the morning, and the Lord said to me, "You are in the third day." I said, "Lord, but it's still dark outside." And He replied, "But it's still a new day!"

Affirmation

I have been launched into the deep and I will embrace my new day, even when it looks familiar. Old things are passed away; behold all things are become new.
—2 Corinthians 5:17

Prophetic Preview

It's time to bring the prophetic out of you. Begin to worship the Lord and get in His presence. Listen closely for His voice and wait for Him to speak.
On the following page, journal your thoughts and impressions. Record every directive given. As heaven is revealed to you, begin to prophetically intercede.
Don't be limited to just words. Allow heaven to communicate to you through visuals. Additional space is provided for you to draw what heaven reveals to you.

Journal

Drawing Space

THE WATCHMAN

THE WATCHMAN

Scripture

"I will stand my watch and set myself on the
rampart and watch to see what He will say to me,
and what I will answer when I am corrected."
—Habakkuk 2:1

Poem

The one that never sleeps operating on God's time clock
Sitting high in the towers of the Spirit keeping watch
Pleading God's mercy, being a go between
Intercepting the enemies plans before they are ever seen
Making declarations and decrees unto the
heavens giving the Lord back His Word
God's will begin to manifest responding to what He has heard
There is great labor and travail
The truth begins to prevail
The effectual fervent prayers avail
The watchmen continue to watch and
pray without ceasing day by day

Releasing the anointing renewing the mind
Watching and praying protecting the vine
They are God's sacred vessels
Earth's greatest intercessors appointed before the world began
This is the life and position of the watchman

Reflection

Being a watchman is a serious prophetic position. In the
Old Testament, the Watchmen sat high on the watchtower
overlooking the vineyard. Vineyards were especially important
because this is where grapes would grow on the vine. Therefore,
watchmen would guard the vine against foxes and thieves
who desired to enter the vineyard. This is where the term
"sound the alarm" comes from. When the enemies came in,
the watchmen would sound the alarm to run the enemy off.
As intercessors, it is particularly important to stand your
watch because those grapes on the vine are future anointings
that need to make it to the winepress to be crushed. You
have a responsibility to cover the next move of God.

Affirmation

I am a powerful prophetic watchman guarding God's vine
and sounding the alarm when it is presented to me.

Prophetic Preview

It's time to bring the prophetic out of you. Begin to
worship the Lord and get in His presence. Listen
closely for His voice and wait for Him to speak.
On the following page, journal your thoughts and
impressions. Record every directive given. As heaven is
revealed to you, begin to prophetically intercede.
Don't be limited to just words. Allow heaven to
communicate to you through visuals. Additional space is
provided for you to draw what heaven reveals to you.

Journal

Drawing Space

RARE BREED

RARE BREED

Scripture

"Will you not revive us again, that your
people may rejoice in you?"
—Psalm 85:6

Poem

The peculiar that moves covertly has to be spiritually discerned
They operate on a frequency of Heaven
that could never be learned
This special ability was given from from above
To demonstrate His power uniquely with love
Some call it an enigma or anomaly because they don't understand
I call it a different way expressing God's plan
This anointing is powerful, with a different presentation
Be watchful and take heed
There is a new sound and power moving upon the earth
That is called Gods Rare Breed.

Reflection

Some would call a rare breed an enigma. However, it may just be mysterious and hard to interpret. A rare breed must be spiritually discerned, as Jesus was when He was resurrected. He was mysterious to the ones He walked with, such as Thomas, who had to put his hands in Jesus' side (John 20:27). He could not look at Jesus and see that it was Him. This breed lives in a realm of ascension. You may feel lonely in this place, but embrace your difference and release what God has given you. This breed is called to release a dimension of God that has not been seen. I release blessings upon you to move in power and authority even when it's misunderstood.

Affirmation

I am a rare breed. I am ready to release God's presence and authority that will change the world.

Prophetic Preview

It's time to bring the prophetic out of you. Begin to worship the Lord and get in His presence. Listen closely for His voice and wait for Him to speak. On the following page, journal your thoughts and impressions. Record every directive given. As heaven is revealed to you, begin to prophetically intercede. Don't be limited to just words. Allow heaven to communicate to you through visuals. Additional space is provided for you to draw what heaven reveals to you.

Journal

"She is a warrior capable of slaying the demons in life. She is a pioneer capable of choosing her own path. She is a trailblazer capable of achieving new horizons. Just give her some time and see her bedazzle the world."

—Avijeet Das

Scripture References

Isaiah 59:19

Isaiah 55:11

Matthew 6:20

Lord God Almighty, I praise You this day and lift
my voice to exalt and reverence Your Holy name.
I praise and releasee an atmosphere for
angels to operate on my behalf.
As I praise, I release Your glory around me that cannot
be penetrated by demonic forces, in Jesus name.
Lord Jesus, cover me in Your blood from the
soles of my feet to the crown of my head.
I come as an ambassador of God, speaking the will of
the Kingdom of Heaven into the earth, in Jesus name.
I declare that every lie of the enemy that has been
enslaving me be exposed in Jesus name.
I prohibit all satanic activity from
operating in every area of my life.
I decree that all demonic powers are
broken in the mighty name of Jesus.
I declare that every flooding of Satan is frustrated
with the standard of the Lord that is lifted.
"No weapon formed against me from the pit of hell
will prosper, and every tongue is being condemned
that rises against me" declares the Word of the Lord.
Every stronghold attempting to hold strong in my life
and atmosphere, I pull you down in Jesus name.

I declare that God will use me day by day
to enforce the laws of the Kingdom.
As His Word is released, it will accomplish what it
was set out to do and never return unto Him void.
Great exploits, manifestations, power, dominion,
and authority shall take its rightful place in
the earth through me, in Jesus name.
May every word be sealed with Your blood,
surrounded by Your Spirit, and received.
In Your name, Lord Jesus,
Amen.

THE ABUNDANT OIL PRESS

THE ABUNDANT OIL PRESS

Scripture

"Then Jesus came with them to a place called Gethsemane, and
said to the disciples, "Sit here while I go and pray over there."
And He took with Him Peter and the two sons of Zebedee, and
He began to be sorrowful and deeply distressed. The He said
to them, "My soul is exceedingly sorrowful, even to death. Stay
her and watch with Me." He went a little farther and fell on His
face, and prayed, saying, "O My Father if it is possible, let this
cup pass from Me: nevertheless, not as I will, but as you will."
—Matthew 26:36-39

Poem

There is a process not known to every man
It shapes and forms us for the Master's Plan
Sometime there is hurt, pain and even abuse
But as we move forward, we become fit for the Father's use
I feel the discomfort of deep thoughts and trails
But I also hear you saying Lord I am here with you my child
The cup that I must drink bitterly with little strength to bear

I hear you whispering in my Spirit, keep going we're almost there
Then You say to me, I see the creation of
beauty that lies in you so full
I smile with satisfaction for this is the coming forth of fresh oil
The Bible shows that Gethsemane was
one of the Lord's greatest test
This is the place of your abundant oil press

Reflection

There is a place in your life where God must press out what
is in you. This place is fully ready to be birthed and must
come out. Christ the Lord, in the Garden of Gethsemane (Oil
Press), went through the process of letting go of His will so
that God's will could be done (surrender). During this time,
Christ was feeling sorrowful, alone, and soon to be betrayed.
He could feel the pressures of the burdens of this world
that would ultimately save you and me. This was a personal
moment for Him, and He did not want to drink from the
bitter cup; He did not want to be forsaken to bear our sins.
Finally, He surrenders and says, nevertheless, not my will, but
Thine be done. Despite all of the burdens we experience for
others, we must surrender them to God. And even though
it feels impossible. The blessing is in the surrender.

Affirmation

Today, I walk in my nevertheless. My surrender
and abundance brings Glory to my Savior!

Prophetic Preview

It's time to bring the prophetic out of you. Begin to worship the Lord and get in His presence. Listen closely for His voice and wait for Him to speak.

On the following page, journal your thoughts and impressions. Record every directive given. As heaven is revealed to you, begin to prophetically intercede.

Don't be limited to just words. Allow heaven to communicate to you through visuals. Additional space is provided for you to draw what heaven reveals to you.

Journal

Drawing Space

NEW WINE

NEW WINE

"And it will come to pass in that day that the mountains shall drip with new wine, the hills shall flow with milk, and all the brooks Judah shall be flooded with water; A fountain shall flow from the house of the Lord and water the valley of acacias."
—Joel 3:18

Poem

New wine is falling from heaven can you see?
Breaking the barriers of apostasy
Many men have fallen away
Jesus says, I am the truth, life and way
No one comes to the Father but by Me
This is eternal victory
I created you specifically to speak and address
My Kingdom coming, putting all spirits to the test
This new wine convicts all error, then leads to truth
The word as it comes forth will rebuke, correct and reproof
As the grapes are crushed and vats overflow

The new wine comes, Christ purpose in full show
I never thought my destiny was divine
But Lord how I thank You for making me new wine

Reflection

New wine is powerful. It needs its own container (wineskin).
If this substance is put into an old wineskin, it will burst. New
wine will destroy old systems; it is a breaker. Nothing old can
withstand it. Remember, the Lord has anointed you as new
wine. This is a divine position at an appointed time. You must
embrace who you are, even when it disrupts your environment.

Affirmation

I have been released as new wine that is effective
and powerful in my sphere of influence.

Prophetic Preview

It's time to bring the prophetic out of you. Begin to
worship the Lord and get in His presence. Listen
closely for His voice and wait for Him to speak.
On the following page, journal your thoughts and
impressions. Record every directive given. As heaven is
revealed to you, begin to prophetically intercede.
Don't be limited to just words. Allow heaven to
communicate to you through visuals. Additional space is
provided for you to draw what heaven reveals to you.

Journal

THE PAINS OF LIFE & THE PLEASURES OF CHRIST

THE PAINS OF LIFE & THE PLEASURES OF CHRIST

Scripture

"Weeping may endure for a night, but joy comes in the morning."
—Psalm 30:5

Poem

Sometimes my pain seems so great
My heart faints and I lose faith
Things that want to live in me,
my pain kills slowly
From rejection, abandonment
and more being revealed
Sometimes I wonder will I ever gain
There is a silent cry within me
I feel so much pain
Then I hear a voice that speaks
Beyond my understanding or intellect
this voice is unique
Its saying weeping may endure for a night

but joy cometh in your morning
I've given you eagles wings
with a new garment that is adorning
Far above life's circumstances
and even the rain
Into a holy abode
let heavens atmosphere bring a change
There are always lessons we learn from this life
But nothing compares to the pleasures of Christ

Reflection

Sometimes, life does not look like what God has ordained
for you. You may experience trauma, death, betrayal,
and things beyond your control. This may begin to shake
your faith, but really, the Lord is producing capacity
and depth in you. Then, He will speak and show you a
solution that shifts the course of your thoughts and life.

Affirmation

My process produces the peaceable fruit of
righteousness in me. (Hebrews 12:11).

Prophetic Preview

It's time to bring the prophetic out of you. Begin to worship the Lord and get in His presence. Listen closely for His voice and wait for Him to speak.

On the following page, journal your thoughts and impressions. Record every directive given. As heaven is revealed to you, begin to prophetically intercede.

Don't be limited to just words. Allow heaven to communicate to you through visuals. Additional space is provided for you to draw what heaven reveals to you.

Journal

Drawing Space

"Becoming unshakeable through this storm."

— Nikki Rowe

Scripture Reference

Micah 7:8-13

Dear Heavenly Father, I stand here with all rights given to me by You, and ask for Your power and authority to be revealed in all the situations prayed for at this time, in Jesus name.
I cover myself and everything pertaining to me with the blood of Jesus Christ, and release the fire of God upon all evil situations concerning myself, family, and ministry in Jesus name.
I place a hedge of protection around everything concerning me, my marriage, and my family. I release angels to encamp round about us in the name of Jesus Christ.
Cause my ears to be sensitive to Your voice. I ask for You to open my ear gate in the Spirt, in the name of Jesus.
Sharpen my discernment and understanding in Jesus name.
According to the Word of God, Lord raise Your standard against every enemy flooding in my life.
God, cause me to have the vision of an eagle to see into the heavenly realms, and behold Your secret things, that I may understand the hour we are in, as the Body of Christ.

According to Micah 7:8 I decree: "Rejoice not
over my falling, I shall arise again, and the Lord
shall be my light where I sit in darkness."
Every hidden disguise of the enemy shall be exposed
in every area of my life and dealt with by warrior
angels assigned to protect me, in Jesus name.
Lord, I bless You for every trial and
tribulation that has caused me to know
and encounter You in another realm.
Oh Lord, thank You for every bondage
and hopeless place, that I may now be
a conduit of Your abundant life.
I declare that I will begin to go through
portals that usher me into another dimension
of revelation in You, in Jesus name.
I command every dry bone to live and receive flesh for
its journey in my life in the name above every name.
I command every Lazarus situation to come forth in my
life with grave clothes removed.
And I seal every word spoken.
In Jesus name,
Amen.

I AM A WARRIOR

I AM A WARRIOR

Scripture

"And they overcame him by the blood of the Lamb and by the word of their testimony, and they did not love their lives to the death."
—Revelation 12:11

Poem

I am a warrior
I overcame the plots and plans of Satan
to destroy me in my infancy
Rejected, abandoned, pushed to the side,
unwanted by my family
I am a warrior because I overcame
abuse and violation of the worst kind
Satan tried to defile my temple
and plant seeds of hopelessness in my mind
I am a warrior that overcame the world's systems
that had me bound and caged
I overcame by the blood

of the Ancient of Days
I am a warrior that realized that Christ chose me
and I accepted Him in my heart
I received eternal life
that would never tear us apart
I am a warrior in Christ Jesus
I win
He has saved my soul
and blotted out my sin

Reflection

I have a testimony; do you? As I look at what the Lord has
brought me through, I understand that I am special to Him—
case and point! Many have had breakdowns and lost their
lives, but I am here today to write and express my heart. I have
endured hardship as a good soldier, which has trained me in the
Spirit. I am a warrior because I have overcome, and so are you.

Affirmation

I declare that I am a warrior, handcrafted and trained by the Lord.

Prophetic Preview

It's time to bring the prophetic out of you. Begin to
worship the Lord and get in His presence. Listen
closely for His voice and wait for Him to speak.

On the following page, journal your thoughts and impressions. Record every directive given. As heaven is revealed to you, begin to prophetically intercede. Don't be limited to just words. Allow heaven to communicate to you through visuals. Additional space is provided for you to draw what heaven reveals to you.

Journal

Drawing Space

WEAPONS OF MASS DESTRUCTION

WEAPONS OF MASS DESTRUCTION

Scripture

"For the weapons of our warfare are not carnal but mighty
in God for pulling down strongholds, casting down
arguments and every high thing that exalts itself against
the knowledge of God, brining every thought into captivity
to the obedience of Christ, And being ready to punish
all disobedience when your obedience is fulfilled."
—2 Corinthians 10:4-6

Poem

Weapons of mass destruction
I am a vessel of war
On the frontline of the battlefield
Uprooting the enemy's tactics from the core
I move in the authority of Heaven,
covered in His almighty blood
The weapons of our warfare are not carnal,
strongholds are destroyed from above
Imaginations have to come subject

to the power of the life-giving Word
I operate from a realm in the spirit
eyes haven't seen nor ears heard
I am covered with the full amour of God
there are watchman on the door post and gates
In this war my head is lifted,
the King of Glory is taking His place
I am fully loaded with ammunition and artillery,
and I send up the war cry
I stand in this place as God's Warrior,
For Christ I live and for Christ I will die
The word says to endure hardship as a good solider,
this was the Apostles instructions
I am clothed with garments of war,
I am a weapon of mass destruction

Reflection

May the power of Jesus Christ rest upon you today because
your life has been established by the Sword of the Lord. He
has given you consistent strategy to live in victory. This makes
you a handcrafted weapon and a force to be reckoned with.

Affirmation

Today, I cast down imaginations that war against
how you created me, Lord. Every place my feet
shall tread, I will possess it (Deuteronomy 11:24),
because I am a weapon of mass destruction.

Prophetic Preview

It's time to bring the prophetic out of you. Begin to worship the Lord and get in His presence. Listen closely for His voice and wait for Him to speak.

On the following page, journal your thoughts and impressions. Record every directive given. As heaven is revealed to you, begin to prophetically intercede.

Don't be limited to just words. Allow heaven to communicate to you through visuals. Additional space is provided for you to draw what heaven reveals to you.

Journal

Drawing Space

TESTS & TRIALS

TESTS & TRIALS

Scripture

"Likewise the Spirit also helps in our weaknesses. For we do not know what we should pray for as we ought, but the Spirit Himself makes intercession for us with groanings which cannot be uttered. Now He who searches the hearts knows what the mind of the Spirit is, because He makes intercession for the saints according to the will of God."
—Romans 8:26-27

Poem

Life has so many pains
The storms that shake your foundation
and the thoughts of your situation begin to rain
I'm told that these things are just a test,
when I think in my flesh, I have no rest
I struggle as I press my way through these trials,
trying to keep the faith as I'm hit with the wiles
The demonic structures that come against my call,
but you Lord have placed a watchman on the wall.

As He prays and stands in the gap,
the devil and his cohorts get caught in a trap
The Word says when the enemy comes in like a flood
a standard is raised by your saving blood
Father, thank you for loving and protecting your child,
I am more than a conqueror in Christ it's just a test and a trail.

Reflection

All things— good or bad— work out for God's Glory. Jesus
Christ intercedes for you and His Holy Spirit protects you
from dangers seen and unseen. See yourself as a champion
and victor! This is how the Lord views His children.
Despite tests and trials, you have everything you need
to overcome and pass the test! Change your thoughts
about your battles because they do not belong to you.

Affirmation

Today, I have a sober mind and I walk in the
victory over every test and trial.

Prophetic Preview

It's time to bring the prophetic out of you. Begin to
worship the Lord and get in His presence. Listen
closely for His voice and wait for Him to speak.
On the following page, journal your thoughts and
impressions. Record every directive given. As heaven is
revealed to you, begin to prophetically intercede.
Don't be limited to just words. Allow heaven to
communicate to you through visuals. Additional space is
provided for you to draw what heaven reveals to you.

Journal

Drawing Space

REVIVAL FIRE IS HERE

REVIVAL FIRE IS HERE

Scripture

"Will you not revive us again, that your
people may rejoice in you?"
—Psalm 85:6

Poem

Revival Fire is here
I see a fire and hear a sound
The earth is shaking
The barrier are breaking down
Revival Fire is here
Psalm 85:6 Wilt thou not revive us again:
that thy people may rejoice in thee
The wind is blowing
Gods people are flowing into position
Revival Fire is here.
There is a mass healing covering the land
God's holy army moving as planned
This power is greater than what we have ever seen

The glory so powerful there is no in between
This presence is weighty and has entered our sphere
Revival Revival Fire is here!!!!!!

Reflection

There is a remnant that carry the torch of revival. God has summoned and released this breed of people at this appointed time. Revival is coming to the land to heal it because we have prayed. 2 Chronicles 7:14 confirms that if God's people who are called by His name would humble themselves and pray, that He would hear from heaven and heal the land. God has given the remnant the supernatural ability to move in great power. Fire will be released and we will be able to see flames in their footsteps. Get ready to release the fire that produces revival. We will see joy again!

Affirmation

I am God's appointed remnant to carry and
release revival fire in the earth!

Prophetic Preview

It's time to bring the prophetic out of you. Begin to
worship the Lord and get in His presence. Listen
closely for His voice and wait for Him to speak.
On the following page, journal your thoughts and
impressions. Record every directive given. As heaven is
revealed to you, begin to prophetically intercede.
Don't be limited to just words. Allow heaven to
communicate to you through visuals. Additional space is
provided for you to draw what heaven reveals to you.

Journal

Drawing Space

"We delight in the beauty of the butterfly, but rarely admit the changes it has gone through to achieve that beauty."
— Maya Angelou

Scripture References

Zechariah 1:17-21
Isaiah 60:2

Heavenly Father, I thank You for power
over all the power of the enemy.
I send torment against everything
that is a torment in my life.
I bind every evil spirit with the power that is in
the resurrection of Jesus Christ and command
them to leave my life in Jesus name.
I bind every principality in the land.
I bind every throne and false wind of Satan that is
blowing across the land and in my atmosphere.
I command them out of my life in
the name of Jesus Christ.
I call for a resurrection into my life.
Everything that has died in my life that should
be a part of my glory— live! I command them
to come alive now, in Jesus name.
May there be a supernatural release of glory upon me.
I condemn, judge, and cast out every evil thing,
circumstance, and situation that comes against
me with the authority that has been given
to me, as a saint of the most high God.

Oh God, arise and scatter every horn set against
my life in the name of Jesus and recreate
my circumstance to receive blessings.
Open my gates of dominion in the name of
Jesus, according to the spirit of prophecy.
In Jesus name,
Amen.

HEALING WATERS

HEALING WATERS

Scripture

"And by the river upon the bank thereof, on this side and
on that side, shall grow all trees for meat, whose leaf shall
not fade, neither shall the fruit thereof be consumed: it shall
bring forth new fruit according to his months, because their
waters they issued out of the sanctuary: and the fruit thereof
shall be for meat, and the leaf thereof for medicine."
—Ezekiel 47:12

Poem

There is healing and restoration for thee,
brining your life full circle into your appointed destiny.
There is a light shining in dark places, God is
raising you up be not afraid of their faces.
There is mending for a damaged soul,
the Lord wants to apply healing balm to make you whole.
There is seven-fold coming back to you, for all
the locust/thief stole is restored a new.

The Lord has turned your captivity, you
now embrace a new reality.
He has always known His plans to prosper you to be,
His holy vessel full of power and abundant life,
living waters rising from your belly overtaking spirits of strife.
The river flows with waters that heal,
Restoration takes place, new strength we feel.
We are covered with the sword and shield.
Revelation of who we are in Christ revealed.
You shall avail more than just the ordinary,
as healing waters flow from your sanctuary.

Reflection

There is depth in your belly; it houses things that live. Healing
is needed in so many areas. You may need physical or emotional
healing. You may need healing from a broken heart, rejection,
abuse, or abandonment. So, allow the Lord to shine His light
into your dark places. If you need physical healing, understand
that He took 39 stripes for you, and by those stripes, you were
already healed. So, receive it! If you need mental healing, "let
[His] mind be in you, which was also in Christ Jesus (Philippines
2:5). Your mind has a spirit that God desires to renew. Ephesians
4:23 says to be renewed in the spirit of your mind. So, God
will heal you from your past pain. Now be restored and watch
your life come full circle. Everything you need is in the river.

Affirmation

I have living water in me; this water is flowing out of me. The blessings of this water heal me from within and catapult me into a new place of freedom in my life.

Prophetic Preview

It's time to bring the prophetic out of you. Begin to worship the Lord and get in His presence. Listen closely for His voice and wait for Him to speak.
On the following page, journal your thoughts and impressions. Record every directive given. As heaven is revealed to you, begin to prophetically intercede.
Don't be limited to just words. Allow heaven to communicate to you through visuals. Additional space is provided for you to draw what heaven reveals to you.

Journal

Drawing Space

THE OPEN DOOR

THE OPEN DOOR

Scripture

"For a great door and effectual is opened unto
me, and there are many adversaries."
—1 Corinthians 16:9

Poem

Lord I thank you for the open door,
the leading of Your Presence is true and sure.
This is a place of access for all to see,
shutting down the snares of the enemy.
This place is great and effective declares the Word,
eyes have not seen, ears have not heard.
This present revelation reveals the new place
Behold all things are new and the old cant be traced.
This place is like no other access we have ever had before,
Lord I praise and lift Your Holy name for
this great and effective door.

Reflection

God has opened a door for you that no man can shut (Revelation 3:8). Rejoice at the opportunity to go through both natural and spiritual doors! There is rapid acceleration in the natural, as well as promotion. Look for it and expect it, spiritually. Expect a greater capacity. It is a kairos moment to go through doors that are unfamiliar, which means you can only operate in a place that Christ can dictate and interpret. Begin to sense a hovering of His Presence over your life, leading you through multiple doors of opportunity. Take a moment to acknowledge the doors that have been opened; you will see the adversaries arise, even the enemy of your soul. But keep your focus on the Lord, just as Peter did when he walked on water. Walk through the door to a place of no return. Pray in the Spirit, and ask the Lord to show you your open doors.

Affirmation

Today, I walk through my God ordained doors and declare that I will never miss His appointed opportunities.

Prophetic Preview

It's time to bring the prophetic out of you. Begin to
worship the Lord and get in His presence. Listen
closely for His voice and wait for Him to speak.
On the following page, journal your thoughts and
impressions. Record every directive given. As heaven is
revealed to you, begin to prophetically intercede.
Don't be limited to just words. Allow heaven to
communicate to you through visuals. Additional space is
provided for you to draw what heaven reveals to you.

Journal

Drawing Space

THE CREATIVE YOU

THE CREATIVE YOU

Scripture

"Therefore, if anyone is in Christ, he is a new creation; old things have passed away; behold, all things have become new."
—2 Corinthians 5:17

Poem

I've made you someone special unique in all the earth
I created you with beauty, spiritual stamina, and self-worth
As My peace surrounds your countenance
beside the waters that are still
I release a fresh anointing which is My perfect will
You are a treasured vessel hidden like a diamond in the rough
Your priceless beauty is shining despite
the journey that's been tough
Old things have passed away and behold
all things have become new
I see the Glory of the Lord, just look at the creative you

Reflection

God has created all of us with unique gifts and talents. These gifts and talents will fuel our assignments on the earth. There is a level of creative measure of Himself that has been given to the believer. My prayer is that you are able to reflect on how creative He has made you. I declare that the Lord begins to stir your creativity. May He download an abundance of revelation from heaven to you that births good success in your life!

Affirmation

I am creative, powerful, beautiful, successful, and gifted, letting my light so shine before men, that my Father in Heaven is continually glorified.

Prophetic Preview

It's time to bring the prophetic out of you. Begin to worship the Lord and get in His presence. Listen closely for His voice and wait for Him to speak. On the following page, journal your thoughts and impressions. Record every directive given. As heaven is revealed to you, begin to prophetically intercede. Don't be limited to just words. Allow heaven to communicate to you through visuals. Additional space is provided for you to draw what heaven reveals to you.

Journal

Drawing Space

GOD'S MELODY

GOD'S MELODY

"Saying with a loud voice: "Worthy is the Lamb who was slain to receive power and riches and wisdom, and strength and honor and glory and blessing!" And every creature which is in heaven and on the earth and under the earth and such as are in the sea, and all that are in them, I heard saying: "Blessing and honor and glory and power be to Him who sits on the throne, and to the Lamb, forever and ever!" Then the four living creatures said, "Amen! And the twenty-four elders fell down and worship Him who lives forever and ever."
—Revelation 5:12-14

Poem

God's melody God's sound
God's masterpiece, God's crown
The angels worship the Lord, they praise and sing
Holy is the Lamb who is worthy of everything
He created you as a sweet sound in His ear
His most holy vessel without a spirit of fear

It brings Him joy as your melody plays
It overtakes and consumes all the adversary's ways
The very reason and person you're a tune
Is to release God's Glory, flourish and to bloom
Into the fullness of your appointed sound
Rooting out, pulling and throwing down
This tune turns into Gods holy symphony
That is why you are God's special melody

Reflection

When I first realized that I was an intercessor, I begin to move by a specific sound in worship. This sound caused me to bow in reverence before God. I would lay out on the floor and put worship music on that had a precise sound. I would start with worship and then go into intercession until the music stopped. After the music stopped, I was in a place that created a unique sound. I was engaging heaven, and there were moments of silence where God overwhelmed me with revelation and His words. What was I doing? I was building an altar to commune with the Father. So, worship Him today and build your altar. Let Him hear your melody.

Affirmation

I am a sound in the earth. My presence makes sounds in the atmosphere that are pleasing to God.

Prophetic Preview

It's time to bring the prophetic out of you. Begin to worship the Lord and get in His presence. Listen closely for His voice and wait for Him to speak.
On the following page, journal your thoughts and impressions. Record every directive given. As heaven is revealed to you, begin to prophetically intercede.
Don't be limited to just words. Allow heaven to communicate to you through visuals. Additional space is provided for you to draw what heaven reveals to you.

Journal

Drawing Space

"I freed a thousand slaves. I could have freed a thousand more if only they knew they were slaves."
— Harriet Tubman

Scripture References

Joshua 11:1-1-21

2 Samuel 5:20

Father, in the name of Jesus, I stand firm in
my position as your servant and ambassador
in the earth and take authority over
everything for which I have jurisdiction.
I come against demonic influence set up to
sabotage my destiny places with the authority
given to me by the Lord Jesus Christ.
I come against flattering tongues that speak
one way in my presence and destructively
out of my sight, in Jesus name.
I frustrate and take authority over the place that
dark kingdoms come together and form their
strength against me in the mighty name of Jesus.
I come against hidden agendas and
falsehood that are set up to distract me, my
family, and ministry in Jesus name.
I cover myself from misperceptions and ask
that You cause those thoughts in others to
line up with the Word of God that has been
established over my life from before the
foundations of the world, in Jesus name.
As my blessings are being released during this prayer,
there will be no demonic interceptions. Blessings

come to me now! Answers manifest yourself now! I
send angels to get you in the mighty name of Jesus.
I prophesy breakthrough in every area of my
life and the lives of my family. I declare that
Baal Perizm (breakthrough) is our continuous
outcome, in the name of Jesus.
I stand in the victory of the finished work of the
Cross. When Christ resurrected, I resurrected
with Him, and He is now seated at the right
hand of the Father, in Christ Jesus.
I declare that every principality, spiritual wickedness,
and evil power is under my feet, I tread upon them.
The Word of God declares that nothing shall by
any means harm or hurt me in Jesus name.
I will not be seduced into gossip and
backbiting. My words will be words of life
and wisdom in the name of Jesus.
I disallow the enemy to isolate me and I frustrate
every evil plan to do so in the mighty name of Jesus.
I break the demonic barriers of suspicion upon
my life, and ask that You, Lord, would cause
Your truth to prevail in all situations.
Establish me by Your Word and increase my blessings.
Lord, open heaven over me and allow Your Glory to
rain down upon my life and my family, in Jesus name.

Cause my life to line up with the destiny and
purpose that You preordained for me.
Lord, You receive all the Glory out of my life.
Angels carry out your functions to make
sure that every prayer is answered, and
the manifestation takes place quickly.
In Jesus Christ's Holy name,
Amen.

EMBRACE YOUR PURPOSE

You are the first to do great things. You must be bold and do what has been instructed of you. The earth is waiting for your forerunning ability to shift the course of what is ordinary. You must wait for your unique instruction from God. Sometimes it's hard to cut a path and develop uninhabited or uncultivated places. Your assignment has no point of reference, just instruction from above. Move into the extraordinary, blaze trails wherever you go, and make openings in the spirit so that others can benefit from the sacrifice of your call. Pioneer on purpose! You are not alone. God is with you. Keep your eyes on Him.

Years ago, the Lord told me to never to look at others who have the same gift as me because the dimension He created my gift to operate within had not been released in the earth yet! So, I instruct you to do the same. Your gift is a coming attraction that will have high demand in your future.

Embrace your uniqueness and move forward with obedience!

ACKNOWLEDGEMENTS

The completion of this book would not be possible without the love of my Heavenly Father and the support of my family. I am grateful for every experience that has shaped me into the bold, God-fearing woman I am today.

I would like to extend a special thank you to my Lord and Savior Jesus Christ. Thank you for leading and guiding me into all truth. Thank you for scribing through me and saving my soul. Words cannot describe how much I love you. You have been so faithful to me.

To my husband, Rodney Bratcher Sr., thank you for inspiring me to do all that God has ordained me to do. You are more than my partner in life; you are my friend and the absolute love of my life. I can't imagine life without you! I love you forever and always.

To our three children, Anthony, Kiané, and Rodney Jr., I love you dearly and thank you for supporting me in every area of my life.

To my mother, Jennifer Stover, who is fighting the good fight of faith and who gave me life — I love you forever.

To Archbishop Ralph L. Dennis— a true father indeed— you believed in me when I struggled to believe in myself. Thank you for unlocking every aspect of my purpose and speaking to my destiny with your keen insight and bold apostolic anointing. I love you!

ABOUT THE AUTHOR

Rhonda R. Bratcher is the founder of Frontline Warriors for Christ International Ministry Inc., an apostolic and prophetic ministry in Baltimore, MD. She is called to be a Kingdom voice that reforms leaders and regions by unveiling God's truth. She is a deeply passionate prophetic intercessor, revivalist, and teacher of the Word of God who operates strongly in deliverance, healing, and worship. Her mandate is to equip the saints by building and releasing strong apostolic ministry teams of intercessors, healers, deliverers, apostles, and prophets who understand spiritual warfare and culture which advances the purposes of the Kingdom of God. She is supported by her husband Rodney Bratcher Sr., her three beautiful children (Anthony, Kaine, and Rodney Jr.), and her three grandchildren (Kamryn, Kyla, and Rodney).

Made in the USA
Monee, IL
25 July 2021

73851113R00085